Marie Bashkirtseff

From Childhood to Girlhood

e-artnow 2020

Marie Bashkirtseff

From Childhood to Girlhood

The Diary of a Young Artist

Translator: Mary J. Safford

e-artnow, 2020
Contact: info@e-artnow.org

ISBN 978-80-273-0870-5

Contents

PREFACE

THE SOUL OF A LITTLE GIRL

Marie Bashkirtseff, beginning at twelve years old, wrote her journal ingenuously, sincerely, amusing us by her whims, thrilling us by her enthusiasms, touching us by her sufferings.

We have gone through these note-books bound in white parchment, slightly discoloured, like the winding sheet in which sleeps a memory, and have already gathered a volume, precious, not because it describes such an entertainment or such an event, but because it reveals the mentality of a young girl.

This time we have been especially interested by the first books, written in a large, unformed hand, dashing, variable, following the successive impressions of a changeful, sensitive nature.

Very few documents exist concerning children, in whom the nineteenth century alone began to interest itself.

In fact the real personality of the child is very secret, for it distrusts these comprehensive and authoritative beings, "grown-up people." And it hides its ironical observations, its dreams, all the ardour of its little soul.

Children play. They have built, with sand and twigs, a fantastic world peopled with their familiar toys: a grey cloth elephant, a multi-coloured duck as big as that white plush bear. And they are in the jungle, tracking, hunting, killing. Then they dance round to a secret rhythm. Stop to look at them, the game will end. The little mouths will become silent. The child will always hide the ingenuous observations it makes with its clear eyes.

Therefore it seems to us very interesting to show a little girl's existence, not told from the distance of past years, but written day by day. Marie Bashkirtseff was a child of precocious intelligence, ardent will, extreme intensity of life. Maurice Barrès defines it sensibly in saying that she had, "when very young, amalgamated five or six exceptional souls in her delicate, already failing body."

The nomad life led by her parents, residences in Paris, London, Nice, Rome, hastened the development of a vivid intelligence.

This little "uprooted" girl accommodated herself to these varied lives with the versatility of children, but she knew how to reserve her personal life of study. It was a strange intellectual solicitude of the little girl living among idle people and dreaming of "becoming somebody famous." And, completely surrounded by refined luxury, she knew how to see the humble folk, whose expressive features she has inscribed in a way not to be forgotten in her pictures.

If this journal reveals a precocious intellect, it preserves-and this is its charm —a spontaneity of childhood-for the little Slav was a bewitching little girl, with rosy cheeks and clear eyes. Has she not evoked all the marvellous imagination of the little ones in these words: "Because I put on an ermine cloak, I imagine that I am a queen"?

Marie's sentimental life has greatly perturbed her biographers. They have accused her of having a cold, indifferent heart. Others, more penetrating, have seen that Marie considered love as a religion for which a god was necessary. Hence her dream as a young girl: "to love a superior being." And she wrote to Maupassant.

Jean Finot has pointed out that there was something "infinitely tragical in the approach from a distance of these two sublime beings already stamped by death." Besides, Marie did not know the novelist.

Another person interested the young girl, Bastien-Lepage. Their double death-struggle drew them together for a moment, and death permanently unites their names in our memory.

So let us not seek the sentimental secret which Marie did not wish to reveal to us. Goncourt tells us the story of that Hokousaï who signed *"An old man crazy to be conspicuous."* Let us think that Marie was also the *young girl crazy to be conspicuous.*

But let us go back to an idyl little known of Marie's twelfth year. The fact itself is not very extraordinary. The little girl is training herself for motherhood by lavishing caresses on wretched papier-mâché baby dolls. She is practising for her part of woman by playing at being in love. Artless little affairs outlined in the catechism, pervaded by the fragrance of incense. Very similar to these appears to us the enthusiasm the little Slav felt for the Duc de H — —. Candid, affectionate little girl, she says deliciously: "I love him, and that is what makes me suffer. Take away this grief, and I shall be a thousand times more unhappy. The pain makes my happiness. I live for it alone. All my thoughts are centred there. The Duc de H — — is my all. I love him so much. That is a very ancient and old-fashioned phrase, since people no longer love."

After such a passage of captivating vivacity, in which work and pleasures inflame this ardent vitality, other days-numerous, alas! have the mere mention of a date followed by a dash. These are the stations of the disease when the charming body was weakening like a dying flower. And there were the alternations of hope, the physicians consulted when at first she believed everything, to doubt, later, all the remedies with which their pity beguiles anxiety, at last the resigned almost certainty:

"And, nevertheless, I am going to die."

Should the shortness of her existence be regretted for Marie? Certainly, thoroughly in love, she would not have found happiness in marriage, which fashionable society too often transforms into a partnership of egotisms, interests, and hypocrisy. But would not maternity have consoled her, affording her a delicious refuge, her who bent patiently over the faces of the very little children, expressed their fleeting occupations, their intent looks?

Sly death did not permit her to finish her destiny, and the little Slav preserves for us her disturbing virgin charm.

In that villa in Nice, where Marie Bashkirtseff lived, clearly appears the vision of a young girl, harmonious in the whiteness of her usual clothing, with a gaze sparkling with ardent life, her who, Maurice Barrès says,[1] "appears to us a representation of the eternal force which calls forth heroes in each generation and that she may seem of sound sense to us, let us cherish her memory under the proud name of Our-Lady who is never satisfied."

RENÉE D'ULMÉS.

NEW JOURNAL OF MARIE BASHKIRTSEFF

JANUARY, 1873

(Marie was then twelve years old.)

I must tell you that ever since Baden I have thought of nothing except the Duc de H——. In the afternoon I studied. I did not go out except for half an hour on the terrace. I am very unhappy to-day. I am in a terrible state of mind; if this keeps on, I don't know what will become of me.

How fortunate people who have no secrets are!

Oh, God, in mercy save me!

The face makes very little difference! People can't love just on account of the face. Of course it does a great deal, but when there is nothing else —. They have been talking about B——. He has exactly my disposition. I am fond of society; he likes to flirt; he likes to see and to be seen; in short, he is pleased with the same things that please me. They say he is a gambler. Oh! dear! What evil genius has changed him!

Perhaps he is in love-hopelessly?

Happy love ought to make us better, but hopeless love! Oh, I believe it must be that!

No, no, he is simply dragged down like so many young men by that terrible gulf. Oh, what an accursed place! How many wretched beings it has made! Oh, fly from it! Take your sons, your husbands, your brothers away from there, or they are lost. B—— is beginning. The Duc de H—— has begun, too, and he will go on, while he might live happily. Live and be useful to society. But he spends his time with wicked men and women. He can do it as long as he has anything, and he used to be immensely rich.

Dr. V—— has said that Mademoiselle C——[2] is ill, that she may live five years or die in three weeks, because she is consumptive. How many misfortunes at once!

If, when I am grown up, I should marry B—— what a life it would be! To stay all alone, that is, surrounded by commonplace men, who will want to flirt with me, and be carried away by the whirl of pleasure. I dream of and wish for all these things, but with a husband I love and who loves me —.

Ah, who would suppose it was little Marie, a girl scarcely twelve years old; who feels all this! But what am I saying? What a dismal thought! I don't even know him, and am already marrying him-how silly I am!

I am really much vexed about all this. I am calmer now. My handwriting shows it. The spontaneous burst of indignation is a little quieted. It is soothing to write or communicate one's ideas to somebody.

B—— isn't worth while. I shall never marry him. If he begs me on his knees, I shall be-oh, I forgot the word —I shall be firm. No, that isn't the word, but I know what I mean. Yet if he loves me very much, very deeply, if he cannot live without me-vain phrases! Do not let us meet. I don't wish to be weak.

I am firm, I will be resolute. I mean to have the Duc de H——. I love him at least. His dissipated life may be forgiven him. But the other-no!

While writing I was interrupted by a noise. I thought some one was going to surprise me. Even if what I have written were not seen, I should blush all the same. Everything I wrote previously now seems nonsense. Yet it is really exactly what I felt. I am calm now. Later I will read it over again. That will bring back the past.

I love the Duc de H — — and I cannot tell him so. Even if I did, he would pay no attention to it. O, God! I pray Thee! When he was here, I had an object in going out, in dressing. But now! I went to the terrace hoping to see him in the distance for at least a second.

O God, relieve my suffering! I can pray to Thee no more. Hear my petition. Thy mercy is so infinite. Thy grace is so great, Thou hast done so many things for me! Thou hast bestowed so many blessings upon me. Thou alone canst inspire him with love for me!

Oh, dear! I imagine him dead, and that nothing can draw him nearer to me. What a terrible thought! I have tears in my eyes, and still more in my heart. I am weeping. If I did not love him I might console myself. He would suit me for a husband in every respect. I love him, and that is what makes me suffer. Take away this anguish, and I shall be a thousand times more miserable. My grief makes my happiness. I live solely for that. All my thoughts, everything is centred there. The Duc de H — — is my all. I love him so much! It is a very old-fashioned phrase, since people no longer love. Women love men for money, and men love women because they are the fashion or on account of their surroundings.

I could not say, "On such or such a day I met a young man whom I liked." I do not know when I noticed him. I cannot even understand these feelings, I cannot find expressions. I will only say, "I do not know when, I do not know how this love has come. It came because it probably had to come." I should like to define this, yet I cannot.

Now, if he were paying me attention, he would think he was doing me honour, but then I should make him see that it is I who honour him by marrying him, because I am giving up all my glory. Yet what happiness can be greater: To have everything-to be a child worshipped by its parents, petted, having all a child can have. Then to be known, admired, sought by the whole world, and have glory and triumph every time one sings. And at last to become a duchess, and to have the duke whom I have loved a long while, and be received and admired by everybody. To be rich on my own account and through my husband; to be able to say that I am not a plebeian by birth, like all the celebrities-that is the life, that is the happiness I desire. If I can become his wife without being a cantatrice, I shall be equally well pleased, but I believe that is the only way I shall be able to attract him.

Oh, if that could be! My God! Thou hast made me find in what way I shall be able to obtain what I ask. Oh! Lord! Aid me, I place all my hopes in Thee. Thou alone canst do all things, canst render me happy. Thou hast made me understand that it is through my voice I can obtain what I seek. Then it is upon my voice that I must fix all my thoughts, I must cultivate, watch, and guard it. I swear to Thee, O Lord, no longer to sing or scream as I used to do.

On leaving the H — —'s, I was wrapped in an ermine cloak. I thought I looked very well. If I became a duchess, a cloak like that would suit me. I am growing too presumptuous. Because I put on an ermine cloak, I imagine that I am a queen.

Monday, our day. We have plenty of callers. I went in only a minute to ask Mamma something, in my character of a little girl. Before entering I looked at myself in the mirror hanging there: I was good-looking, rosy, fair, pretty.

Suppose I should write everything I think and everything I intend to do when I grow up, everything I mean to forget, and everything that is extraordinary? A dinner service of transparent glass. On one side a certain costume and arrangement of the hair; on the other side a different costume and a different arrangement of the hair, so that on one side I shall be one person, and on the other side another. To give a dinner by letters. I have determined to end this book, for extravagant ideas rarely come to me in these days.

March 14th, 1873.

I saw Madame V —— on the Promenade. I was so glad, not on her own account-yes, a little, but because all these people remind me of Baden.

There I could see the Duc, because he spent nearly all his time out of doors, but it did me no good, for I was a child. If I could be at Baden *now* for a summer! O, dear! When I think that Grandpapa made his acquaintance in a shop. If I could have foreseen, I should have continued that acquaintance.

I think only of him, I pray God to keep every trouble from him, protect, preserve him from every danger.

All this time people talk about the Duc de H —— and it pleases me immensely, if I don't blush.

At last I can enjoy some bright weather on the Promenade. I have seen everybody, and I am happy. An hour driving, then walking, but the rain surprised us.

In the evening we went to the theatre, which was filled with fashionable people. The W —
—'s were next to us. I talked about the springs, horses, etc. To-day I have been reflecting. Not a moment must be lost, every instant must be spent in study. Sometimes (I am ashamed to confess it) I hurry through my lessons without understanding them, in order to finish more quickly, and I am glad when lessons are given me to review because, during the following days, I shall have less to do.

I don't intend to behave so any longer. I must finish what I am learning quickly, that I may begin serious studies, like those of men, and occupy myself more with music, commence lessons on the harp and singing. These are great plans. They are sensible ones, too. Are they not?

March 30th, 1873.

I have been dreaming of the Duc de H ——. He wore three jackets of the queerest cut, and was at our house to look at my pictures. He admired them, and I talked with him. I was very much agitated, and could scarcely conceal it. He talked with me very pleasantly, and spoke of B ——. He said:

"I was talking with her. I made her sit down and I spoke of you."

Oh! he talked to her about me, and it was on my account that he spoke to her! How happy I am! At last my prayer is granted! Then he brought some kind of paper or something, I don't know exactly what, to ask for an address to get clothes, I believe. He was in the large drawing-room, talked to me in low tones, encouraged me by his frank manners, then I saw mountains on the pictures at which he was looking. It is strange that I felt nothing extraordinary, and I was less excited than when I am awake.

I was happy, I was calm and content.

These transports overwhelm me at the mere sight of his name, for I am not sure of my happiness, and I ardently desire it. But when we have what we desire and love, we are calm. So, in my dream I was calm, for I no longer had anything to desire. I said nothing, in order not to interrupt my happiness. I let myself go gently and quietly.

What was my surprise to find, on waking, that all this happiness was only a dream! I spoke of it to members of the family, I laughed at myself, to conceal my joy and my love for him. He talked with me tenderly. Not exactly, but I know what I mean. He was not precisely like himself, smaller and not so handsome. I thought I had reached port, but, on waking, I find myself in the open sea and in the midst of the tempest, as I was yesterday and shall be for a long time, perhaps, until he comes to lead me on board. That is a commonplace phrase, but it well expresses what I wish to say and I use it. Then an hour's practice on the piano. Then to the Promenade. Mademoiselle de G —— wore a broad-brimmed grey felt hat, turned up at one side. O, how I would like a hat like that! It is so graceful. I would like a hat like that, and the same style of gown. It brings back the young ladies of former days, tall, well-formed, slender, beautiful. One would say that I am raving over a gown as I do over the man I love.

Tuesday, April 8th.

I had a geography lesson to-day. While looking for a city in America, my eyes were attracted by this tragical name: H — — island in the Arctic Ocean. It seemed as if a thunderbolt had struck me, I did not feel the earth under my feet. My heart beat violently, I was completely upset. Can I doubt that I love him? If he knew it! But, with God's assistance he will know it some day. God is so good. He has given me all I have possessed up to the present moment.

* * * * *

Mademoiselle C — — scolded me to-day because people looked at me too much on the Promenade. While returning from church we talked about religion-then went on to the Duc de H — —. Mademoiselle C — — said:

"What associates he has! To-day he is with the H — —'s."

I want to describe conversations better. The Duc de H — — was discussed. I defended him warmly, but I have seen that I went too far.

Good Friday.

At church, when we went to kiss the tomb of Christ, I looked at all the faces and suddenly *his* appeared as if he were there in person. Never has it presented itself so distinctly. This time I saw it as if it were himself. At this apparition my heart beat violently, and I began to pray. I wanted to recall this beloved face, but in vain. I no longer see it.

At this vision, an idea came to me. There were a great many flowers near the tomb. I took a daisy. The flower is holy, it was near our Saviour. It will tell me whether our desires will be realised. With a throbbing heart, I pulled off petal after petal. Yes-no —O, God! I thank Thee! I believe this prediction, it is holy!

I don't want to wait any longer. I shall die if I stay in this furnace. It is too warm. Knock, and it shall be opened unto you. I believe that, it is my consolation. We are going to Vienna Saturday, but Mamma will stay. There is no pleasure without pain. That is a great truth. So we shall start Saturday, I, my aunt, Dina, and Paul.

During the journey the most open-hearted gaiety did not cease to reign among us. O, how disagreeable Italy is on account of the Italians, how dirty they are! We wanted to take a bath, and I did not expect to have such luck in an Italian hotel in Genoa. I was greatly surprised when they brought it to me.

At ten o'clock we at last reached our destination. We went to the Grand Hotel. Everything is magnificent. I am pleased with it. I wanted to take a bath. It is too late.

We all went to the Exposition and saw a part of Germany, England, and France. The costumes were heavenly.

That is the way I shall dress later. How beautiful art can render finery! I adore dress, because it will mate me pretty and give pleasure to the man I love, and I shall be happy. Then dress bestows Paradise upon earth.

The Russian pavilion is extremely beautiful, everything is fine. We breakfasted at the Russian restaurant. It is neither restaurant nor Russian. It is a sort of German beer-hall. The servants are dressed in red, a perfect caricature. It isn't surprising that Russians should be taken for Turks. I am having a good time to-day. The first two it seemed as though I was in a lethargy. That happens to me sometimes. It is over now. The Italian statues are very original. There are some remarkable expressions of face.

Say what you like, our native land is always our native land. Everything that is Russian in the pavilion is beautiful. I looked eagerly. There were Russian names on the goods. My eyes filled with tears.

At seven o'clock, we went to hear the band. There were a great many people, the music was very captivating, thoroughly Viennese. When this orchestra stopped, another began. All sorts of persons, members of the imperial family, fashionable ladies, young dandies, a whirl of gaiety.

The Viennese climate is delicious, not like Nice, which is burning hot in summer.

At last! We are leaving! We are in the train. There is no time to collect one's thoughts. We pass cities, cottages, huts, and in each dwelling people are talking, loving, quarrelling, bestirring themselves. Every human being whom we see, smaller than a fly, has his joys and sorrows. We are talking so much of Baden. We shall pass through it to-morrow. I should like to go there.

At five o'clock in the morning I was waked. We were approaching Paris. I dressed quickly, but there were fifty minutes to spare. We went to the Grand Hotel.

Paris is comical in the morning. Nothing to be seen except butchers, pastry cooks, boot-makers, restaurant keepers, opening and cleaning their shops.

Toward noon, I was not only settled, but ready to go out. In Paris I am at home, everything interests me; instead of being lazy, I am in too great a hurry. I should like not only to walk, but to fly. I wanted to make myself believe that there was society in Vienna, but that is impossible. The hotel is full of a very good sort of English people. We are going to Ferry's. I took the address in Vienna. We shall buy two pairs of boots, one black, the other yellow.

We went on foot. I ordered some gloves. I dress myself. My allowance is 2,500 francs a year. I received 1,000 francs. Then we took a cab and went to Laferrière's. I ordered a tête-de-nègre costume (three hundred francs).

"Here comes the Duc de H — —. Don't jump out of the carriage." My aunt looked at me sternly. This evening I asked myself if I really did love the Duc, or if it was imagination. I have thought of him so much that I fancy things which do not exist — I might marry somebody else. I imagine myself the wife of another. He speaks to me. Oh! no, no! I should die of horror! All other men disgust me. In the street, at the theatre, I can endure them, but to imagine that a man may kiss my hand drives me wild!

I don't express myself well, I never know how to explain myself, but I understand my own feelings.

To-night we are going to the theatre. This is Paris! I can't believe that I am here. This is the city from which all the books are taken. All the books are about Paris, its salons, its theatres, it is the perfection of everything.

At last I have found what I have desired without knowing it. To live is Paris-Paris means to live!

I was tormenting myself because I did not know what I wanted. Now I see it before me. I know what I want. To move from Nice to Paris. To have an apartment, furnish it, have horses as we do in Nice. To go into society through the Russian ambassador. That, that is what I want.

How happy we are when we know what we want! But an idea has come to me —I believe I am ugly. It is frightful!

To-day is the first time we have seen the Bois, the Jardin d'Acclimatation, and the Trocadéro, from which we had a view of all Paris. Really, I have never in my life beheld anything so beautiful as the Bois de Boulogne. It is not a wild beauty, but it is elegant, sumptuous.

Since Toulon, I have been the prey of a great sorrow. All places are indifferent to me, except Paris, which I adore, and Nice.

At last! We have reached this spot. Princess G——and W——met us.

Mamma was not there. We asked for her and were told that she was a little indisposed. The truth is that she fell out of bed and hurt her leg. We arrived. I made her sit in the dining-room. An arrival is always confused. People talk and answer, all speaking at once.

During my absence a little negro boy was engaged, who will go out with the carriage. I cannot look through the window. I can't bear this pale foliage, this red earth, this heavy atmosphere! So Mamma said that we will stay in Paris! Heaven be praised!

We were summoned to dinner, but first I arranged my room. Then I went back to the drawing-room, where Mamma was lying. We talked and laughed, I told what I had seen, in short, we discussed everything. I fear Mamma will be seriously ill. I shall pray to God for her. I am glad to be back in my chamber, it is pretty. To-morrow I mean to have my bed all in white. That will be lovely.

I regard Nice as an exile. I intend to occupy myself specially in arranging the days and hours of tutors.

With winter will come society, with society, gaiety. It will not be Nice, but a little Paris. And the Races! Nice has its good side. All the same, the six or seven months which must be spent there seem like a sea I must cross without turning my eyes from the light-house which guides me. I do not expect to approach, no, I only hope to see this land, and the sole thing which gives me resolution and strength to live until next year. Afterward! Really, I know nothing about it! But I hope, I believe in God, in His divine goodness, that is why I don't lose courage. Whoever lives under His protection will find repose in the mercy of the Omnipotent One. He will cover thee with His wings. Under their shelter thou wilt be in safety. His truth will be thy shield, thou wilt fear neither the arrows that fly by night; nor the pestilence that wastes by day! I cannot express how deeply I am moved and how grateful I am for God's goodness toward me.

September 12th, 1873.

This morning I made a scene with Mamma and my aunt. I could stand it no longer, the bottle had to be opened, there was too much gas in it. I wept. It lasted two hours and a half.

I asked forgiveness. Just at that moment some one said that a house on the Rue de France was burning. I ran to see it. We were all at the windows. The carriages were brought from the stables, women came out carrying children. The building was not yet in flames. There was a courtyard surrounded by four sheds filled with hay. The fire flared high, but the people in Nice are always the same. They do nothing to subdue it, only stand at a distance to enjoy the spectacle.

Oh! if it were in Russia, it would have been extinguished long ago. Our fire engines are terrible when they are heard a league away, every quarter has one. The firemen in golden helmets and lots of little bells. (The noise the Duc de H — —'s carriage makes coming from a distance reminds me of the fire engines.)

At last, after half an hour, a cart arrived, dragged by ten men, what a mere nothing! And four soldiers with guns.

No doubt they were going to extinguish the fire with them! But it was out before they came.

So I return to what I was saying: A complete reform in my costume and character, I will become kind, pleasant, gentle. I will try to be the good genius of the house.

I want to make myself loved and esteemed by every one, from the meanest beggar to the duke and king. This is the promise I make to God. Since I desire so great a happiness, I must deserve it. That is the way I hope to obtain it.

Therefore I make a solemn vow to God that I will do what I say. If I fail once in my oath, I shall lose everything. I will address myself to the Holy Virgin and pray her, with Her Son, to guide and protect me.

I rose at five o'clock to-day. I have worked well, I am satisfied with myself. How happy we are when we are content with ourselves! All the rest matters little; we find everything, satisfactory, we are happy. My happiness depends upon myself. I have only to study well.

September 15th, 1873.

I spoke Italian to-day for the first time. Poor M. (my professor) almost fell in a faint, or threw himself out of the window. I can say that I speak English, French, Italian, and am learning German and Latin. I am studying seriously. Day before yesterday I took my first lesson in physics. Oh, how well pleased with myself I am!

I have received the *Derby*. I found a number of horses entered by the Duc de H——. The races at Baden! How I should like to be there. Nothing prevents me, but I will not go. I must study. And with a heavy heart I read of the horse races. I calm myself with great difficulty and comfort myself by saying: "Let us study; our turn will come, if it is God's will."

I have read this journal. My eyes are glittering, my hands are frozen. There is no doubt of it. I adore, I adore-horses. They are my life, my soul, my happiness. By chance I shook my whip. There was the same hissing sound as at the races. I jumped. I no longer know where I am. Come; it mustn't be talked about.

September 20th.

Only at five o'clock I am free, and I am going to the city with the Princess and Dina. In the French lesson I read Sacred History, the Ten Commandments of God. It says we must not make unto ourselves graven images of anything that is in the heavens. The Latins and the Greeks were wrong, they were idolaters who worshipped statues and paintings. I, too, am very far from following this method. I believe in God, our Saviour, the Virgin, and I honour some of the saints, not all, for there are some that are manufactured like plum cakes. May God forgive this reasoning if it is wrong. But in my simple mind this is the way things are and I cannot change them.

Shall I ever believe that God has commanded a tabernacle to be built to have His oracle heard from the ark in it? No, no! God is too great, too sublime for these unbearable Pagan follies. I worship God in everything. People can pray everywhere, and He is everywhere present.

I went to the city for a turn on the Promenade. In the evening we played kings again, but the game isn't sufficiently interesting. We played like amateurs. For all that I had a good time and laughed heartily.

G —— came and —I no longer remember in what connection-said that human beings are degenerate monkeys. He is a little fellow who gets his ideas from Uncle N —— .

"Then," I said to him, "you don't believe in God?" He: "I can believe only what I understand."

Oh, the horrid fool! All the boys who are beginning to grow moustaches think like that. They are simpletons who believe that women cannot reason and understand. They regard them as dolls who talk without knowing what they are saying. With a patronising manner they let them go on. He has doubtless read some book he did not understand, whose passages he recites. He proves that God could not create because at the poles bones and frozen plants have been found. Then these lived, and now there are none.

I say nothing against that. But was not our earth convulsed by various revolutions before the creation of man? We do not take literally the statement that God created the world in six days. The elements were formed during ages and ages. But can we deny God when we look at the sky, the trees, and men themselves? Would we not say that there is a hand which directs, punishes, and rewards-the hand of God?

October 5th.

We went with Paul to a secluded part of the garden to shoot. My hands trembled a little when, for the first time in my life, I took a loaded gun, especially because Mamma was so frightened. I chose a pumpkin twenty paces away for a target, and shot capitally. The whole charge was in the pumpkin. The second time I fired at a piece of paper twenty centimetres square, again I hit, and a third time a leaf. Then I grew very proud and smiling. All fear disappeared and it seems as if I had courage enough to go to war.

I carried the pumpkin, the paper, and the leaf in triumph to show to Mamma, who is very proud of me.

Really, what harm is there in shooting? I need not become on that account one of those detestable men-women with spectacles, masculine coats, and canes. To fire a gun will not prevent my being gentle, lovable, graceful, slender, vaporous (if I may use the word), and pretty.

While shooting I am a man; in the water a fish; on horseback a jockey; in a carriage a young girl; at an evening entertainment a charming woman; at a ball a dancer; at a concert a nightingale with notes extra low and high like a violin. I have something in my throat which penetrates the soul, and makes the heart leap.

Seeing me with the gun, no one would imagine I could be indolent and languishing at home. Yet, sometimes, when I undress in the evening, I put on a long black cloak which half covers me and sit down in an armchair. I seem so weak, so graceful (which I am in reality) that again no one would imagine I could shoot.

I am a rarity. I shall be highly educated, *if God wills that I should live and blesses me.* I am perfectly formed, my face is pretty enough, I have a magnificent voice, intellect, and I shall be, withal, a woman. Happy the man who will have me. He will possess the earthly Paradise! Provided that he knows how to appreciate me!

I lack everything here, and yet I adore Nice. We always love what does not love. *Sic factae sumus.* Everywhere else I am visiting, at Nice I am at home, and the proverb says: However well off we may be while visiting, we are better off at home. Nice! Nice! Thou ingrate!

I adore Nice and admire it from my window. I am happy and animated. Why? I don't know. After all-Ah! let me alone! The cards tell the truth, I believe in the cards; they have always said yes to me. I must have an occupation, I am of a warlike disposition. I am ready for everything. I ask only an idea. No doubt I shall be depressed to-morrow, for this evening I am certainly on stilts.

The tower clock is striking nine. Lovely tower; lovely I! Ah! H — —.

October 8th, 1875.

We went to N — —'s. The good woman vexed and made me laugh at the same time.

"The first thing to be done in Rome," said Mamma, "is to get teachers of singing and painting."

"Yes," I replied, "and I am going to visit the galleries."

"But what will you do there?" asked Madame S — —.

"Why, copy, study."

"Oh, but you are so far from that point," she said earnestly.

You understand, this foolish woman judges me in that way; but pshaw. What do I care? Yet put yourself in my place, and you will comprehend my annoyance, my irritation.

The good God is cruel. He gives me nothing. To ask the simplest, the most possible thing, to ask it as a mercy, as a happiness, to believe in God, to pray to Him, and to have nothing! Oh! I can see people scoffing at me because I bring God into everything. The poorest thing, by resistance, gains value! My ugly temper gives importance to everything. No, frankly, I must become sensible and mount on my pedestal, raise myself above my troubles. Has it ever happened that everything goes wrong with you? The hair dresses badly, the hat tilts every minute, the flounce on my skirt tears each step I take, pebbles get into my slippers, cutting through my stockings, and prick my feet.

I returned exasperated, and that horrid dog, F — —, leaped joyfully upon me. I went upstairs and it pursued me with its caresses. I kept my patience, but when I reached my room I gave it a kick, and it ran howling under my bed, but after a couple of minutes came back, wagging its tail, and looking at me as if asking my pardon. Oh, the dog! the dog!

No, never shall I be understood!

I should like to have whoever reads my words be myself for an instant in order to understand me, people cannot comprehend what they do not feel, to do so it is necessary to be myself! —and also myself in my lucid moments.

M — — is seventeen to-day, and we lunched at W — —'s. I was horribly bored. Imagine running down a long corridor, so long that you cannot see the end, springing forward and finding only a delusion, coming with your outstretched hands against a wall. That is I!

I rate myself above everything, and the idea that I am placed on the same level with any one, that people do not consider me different from the rest of the world, the bare idea makes me angry. I wish them to forget, to trample everything under foot, to scorn and destroy all that has preceded me —I desire that there should be nothing before, nothing after-except the remembrance of me. Then only I should be content.

When an opportunity offers, I will express my meaning fully.

* * * * *

I went out with neither pleasure nor eagerness. N — — and her children were going to walk, and we enlarged their party.

"Ah! if you knew how I have treated the human race this morning," I said to M — — in answer to a remark I no longer remember.

"Ah! if you knew how little it cares! it is a matter of no importance," replied M — —, very wittily.

How dreary it is to have nobody to care for!

My head is heavy and my eyes are closing, yet at the same time I want to write more, the pen glides easily over the paper and, though I might have nothing to say, I go on for the pleasure of filling the white pages and hearing the pleasant scratching of the pen.

> "My head is heavy and my eyelids close,
> Yet still my gliding pen I will not stay,
> Fain would I tell all my heart's joys and woes,

I am not successful with serious poetry.

Sunday, October 10th, 1875.

I was going to talk with my aunt, but why appeal to human beings? What can men do? God alone can help! God does not hear me! Just God! Holy Virgin! Jesus! I am not worthy to be heard, but I pray you for it on my knees, I pray so earnestly! Is not prayer a merit, however small it may be? Do not the most unworthy obtain what they ask through prayer? Is it nothing to believe and to turn to God? And though I should write until to-morrow I could say nothing but the words:

"My God, have pity on me!"

* * * * *

I who thought I must succeed in everything, see that I am failing everywhere. I shall never console myself for it. How everything in this world repeats itself! I went lately to the Aquaviva terrace and looked to the right. It was in winter, and the mist was gathering on the Promenade. I saw the Duc de H —— go into G ——'s, and now it is precisely the same thing, only then I ordered myself to love him, and now I forbid myself to love.

Then I was crazy over the man; now he interests me because he looked at me.

In a word, why and how? What do the reasons matter? I do not love him. Oh, but I am so provoked! "Come," I said, "rouse yourself, I won't cry about that."

To straighten myself, throw back my head, smile scornfully, then indifferently, and that is all; moisten the ropes, as they did in moving the obelisk of Sixtus Quintus, and I shall be on my pedestal-and I have not an instant's strength. I preferred to stay in my armchair and murmur:

"I fail in everything now."

Confess, you who will read these lines, am I a man? Confess that I have reason to be angry over it.

I, the queen, the goddess. I, who should be worshipped kneeling; I, who do not want to move my little finger lest I should bestow too much honour; I with my ideas; I with my ambition; I with my pride! I confess that, after having seen him go into G ——'s like a master, I feel a sort of respect for him; he acts the duke.

This evening "*Alice de Nevers,*" a comic opera by Hervé, was given for the first time. Our box had been engaged a long while, first proscenium at the right. I was dressed with more care than usual; hair arranged in Marie Antoinette style, without the powder. The whole was drawn up, even the fringe in front. I left only a few little locks at each side. My beautiful white forehead, thus bared, gave me a royal air, and at the back I let two curls hang, waved just at the end.

Gown of dove-grey taffeta and a white fichu. In short, Marie Antoinette in miniature. I felt well satisfied, and gazed at the base multitude from the height of my grandeur. Lighting *a giorno.* I was looked at quite enough.

He could not help staring at me like the rest. Everybody came to our box.

At every intermission I went to the back, so that I would not have to turn my head at each visit. Just as the curtain was rising the Prefect's son and A —— entered our box. I received them with perfect ease; he has a foreign air.

"What, Mademoiselle, are you really going away?"

"Oh, yes, Monsieur."

"No, no," he said, as if he had been pricked by a pin, "Mademoiselle shall not go."

I did not deign to answer. I was courteous, agreeable, but cold. He turned and asked me if I always gave trouble.

"Yes, always."

* * * * *

We are going to the S ——'s. I do not see M ——. She is shut up at home. This is what has happened-during the two months since the C —— family arrived from Mexico, he has no longer written to her.

I know that people who say what I have just said are not popular. We prefer those who, like Dina, veil what they know by a false sentiment of sham delicacy and misplaced pity.

Listen carefully to these commonplace, but true words. C — — deserts you. Write him a letter full of pride and withdraw with honour.

I am very sorry for M — —. C — —will leave Europe in three days.

Poor M — —. This is what it means to love with the heart. I understood at once when she told me that C — — had not written to her for so long. On account of anonymous letters he received; because he thought that he no longer loved her. I instantly comprehended his object. I am frantic for her, when I think what a satisfied face the booby will take with him to Mexico! And that poor girl has been crying ever since this morning. I am pleased. I foresaw everything, we must hold ourselves proudly, especially when the man wants to draw back. He invents excuses, and the poor woman believes she is deserving of reproach, and this, that, and the other thing, while in reality she has no cause for blaming herself. I always try to protect myself against every affront.

"Yes," said Mamma, "I was told that you received him yesterday from the summit of your grandeur."

"Not only yesterday," my aunt interrupted, "but for a long time past."

"That is true," I replied; "otherwise I should never console myself, for he has wounded me by confounding me with other young ladies."

"How glad I am that we have no C — — in our house," remarked Mamma. "My daughter is pure and free from any love."

"Oh! oh!" said my aunt.

* * * * *

Oh, women, women, you will always be the same.

Learn to behave yourselves, wretched sex! See how man marches straight on, without fear, without reproach, and without being afraid of wounding you; he abuses you, and you endure and bow before it. Oh, you men, if you read this, know that I am grieved to the bottom of my heart to allow you so much importance, but it would be both bad taste and bad tactics to decry your worth; the value of our enemies enhances our own. What credit is it to conquer dunces? Know, you who wear trousers, know that in me you have a foe. I take pleasure in magnifying you men in order to maintain in myself the noble ardour which animates me.

Saturday, October 23d, 1875.

I forgot to tell my yesterday's dream. I saw some mice, against which I threw cats that choked them. Then these mice became serpents and went into their holes, while the cats rushed upon me, especially one that scratched my right leg. It is a bad dream. Ah! yes; malediction! I see that there is nothing good for me in this world. Why do you want to live when everything fails, everything goes wrong? We have courage up to a certain point, we make ourselves bold, we hope, but a moment comes when we have strength no longer.

Well! Jeer at me, you hardened people. What! you will say, you dare to utter such words, when your mother is living, when you have an aunt who worships you, a mother who obeys you, a fortune at your command, when you are neither infirm nor ill. You are tempting God.

That is what you will tell me, and I shall answer that life is made up of little things as the body is formed of molecules. When all the molecules decay and go to the Old Nick, the body can no longer live. It is the same with life when all that composes it, colours it, makes it lovable, is lacking, turns out badly, when everything escapes, when not the slightest wish is realised, when everything vanishes, everything deceives. No, to go on in this way is impossible. So I believe that God will recall me soon. It is not in vain that two mirrors were broken this year. People will say that when we are young, we often feel a desire to die, but that is nonsense. I have no desire to die; but I foresee my own death, for a life so useless, so miserable, cannot last.

I have interrupted myself ten times to weep and to think of this summer; when I compare it with the present I am thoroughly wretched. How many lost illusions! What hopes deceived! And I am rid of them. I was going to say that my heart is torn, but it is not true; my heart is whole, my mind is embittered, and deceptions destroy man. Let us surround our hearts with triple brass. I will trouble myself no more about this man. I will no longer think of him, I will no longer speak of him as before, I forbid myself to do it.

October 24th, 1875.

I boasted of my conduct yesterday; there was no reason for it; if I appeared indifferent it was because I was indifferent. These people don't know how to talk; the Arts, history, one doesn't even hear their names. I feel that I am gradually growing stupid. I am doing nothing. I want to go to Rome-to take up my lessons again. I am bored. I feel myself being gradually enveloped in the spider's web which covers everything here, but I am struggling, I am reading.

At the theatre P — — with R — —, her good friend, as they say in Nice, began to yawn when she saw all the people in our box.

Why do women yawn when they are jealous and curious? My mother has noticed it a hundred times, and I, too, in my short life.

Wretched feminine position! Men have all the privileges, women have only that of waiting their good pleasure.

I should be quite proud if I could make myself really loved by this man.

Wild, reckless, ruined, vicious, fickle, brutalised by association with wicked women! His feelings of delicacy, of true love, of virtue, which are the bloom of the human heart, have been early swept away from him. The desire for money holds the first place, money to lead a gay life, to support the riffraff he has in his train.

How much women are to be pitied! It is the man who first takes notice, it is the man who asks to be introduced, it is the man who makes the first advances, it is the man who gives the invitation to dance, it is the man who pays attention, it is the man who offers marriage. The woman is like this paper, this nice paper on which we write whatever we please. God does not hear me, yet I will not doubt God. Often a desire to do it seizes possession of me, but I am very quickly punished.

Pshaw! Life is an ugly thing!

* * * * *

Before dinner we went to walk, it was wonderful moonlight. I said a thousand foolish things to O — —, and if Dina and M — — were as crazy as we, a great scandal would have happened, for we wanted to dance a ring around a priest who was passing.

O — — is writing a novel, it appears. After dinner we went in search of her; I shut myself up with her, and the good girl read it. But at the second page I stopped her and proposed that we should write one together. I gave the idea, everything, everything, and the girl imagines she is composing too. It would be the story of Dumas with the *Tour de Nesle*, but I shall not assert my rights, I am giving her a love scene for to-morrow. She makes no pretensions, and asks for ideas, details, and love scenes with perfect simplicity.

As for me, I set to work and, at one dash, wrote the first chapter, in which my hero bursts open a door and leaps through the window.

People are doing me the honour to busy themselves very much about me, to gossip a great deal over me. Haven't I always desired it?

My journal is suffering because I have begun to write a novel, and I shall succeed. Thank Heaven, I am capable of doing everything I wish. Two chapters in two days is going on finely. I have read it to Dina, and my story interests her. But I am able to judge for myself personally, and I believe it will go.

While we were walking, surrounded by a group of young men, I was happy, proud, and of what? I am little and vain; I took good care to express a wish to return to the carriage, before my cavaliers desired to leave. They even begged me to take another turn. That was all right. They escorted me to the landau.

Monday, November 15th, 1875.

All day long the day of the opera I was restless.

At half past eight o'clock we set off. I was dressed in a white muslin gown, a plain skirt with a wide ruche around the bottom, Marie Stuart waist, and hair arranged to match the costume. A very pretty auditorium. Everybody admired me. Toward the middle of the entertainment, I began to feel as lovely as possible. In going out I passed between two rows of gentlemen who stared at me till their eyes bulged, and they didn't think me bad-looking, one could see that. My heart swelled with pride and joy. Léonie came to undress me, but I sent her away and shut myself up. As I entered I suddenly saw myself in the glass. I looked like a queen, a portrait that had come down from its frame. I no longer had to say: "Ah! if I dressed as people used to do —" I *was* dressed as people used to do. I was beautiful.

It always seems as if others did not see me as I am. How unfortunate that, instead of these little black letters, I could not trace my portrait as I was-my wonderful complexion, my golden hair, my eyes so dark at night, my mouth, my figure! Those who saw me know how I looked.

While remaining simple, as suits one of my age, barely beyond childhood, I was gowned like a grown person. That is where the difficulty lies-to be like a grown person and yet not extravagant and overdressed.

Later I felt very unhappy and began to sing: "Knowst thou the land?" and fell on my knees, weeping. Why? It is a relief to lie on the ground. Because, in the last scene, a love scene, P —— had in her voice-it gave one a thrill —I would die for the truth-and joyfully.

This is it, he who slays with the sword shall perish by the sword.

It seems as if I had loved. I feel in despair; I don't know why, but it was a torturing feeling and made me weep.

Tuesday, November 16th, 1875.

I left Nice to-day with my aunt, I was ready to cry every instant.

"Do you want a pillow?" she asked.

"No."

"Are you ill?"

"No."

"But you look so pale."

"I am tired."

"You must be ill; where do you feel pain?"

"Everywhere! —Come, Aunt, don't disturb me, I am composing."

"Ah!"

"Oh! there is nothing like the rolling of a carriage to give ideas."

"Aha! That's different; well, well, I didn't know."

And she left me to compose at my ease. Then, after a silence:

"Why did A —— turn so pale when P —— began to sing: 'Knowst thou the land?'"

"How could you have seen? For my part, I can never notice whether a person turns pale or blushes."

"Yes, you, because you can't see at a distance, but I can. He turned as white as a sheet when she sang: 'There would I fain live!'"

"I saw nothing."

Wednesday, November 17th, 1875.

Many things have changed since Monday. I don't wish to die, no matter where and no matter how, and I have since been ashamed of myself. I meant to trifle with the man, and it seems as if the man was trifling with me. This insult, joined to the wrath I feel for my weakness Monday, makes me detest him.

At six o'clock we arrived without having secured any accommodations at the Grand Hotel, so we took rooms at the Hôtel Splendide.

"Is it worth while to choose for a hero a miserable Nice scamp like that A — —?" said my aunt, "and to write a lot of stuff about him?"

Certainly my aunt understands nothing of the matter, and that is very fortunate. I do think of him, and yet if he loved me, I would not consent to be his wife. No one in the household considered him a suitable match. They noticed him because I was interested in him. They talked about him because they saw it gave me pleasure, yet if I said I wanted to marry him they would think me crazy, would raise a loud outcry, for they are dreaming of a throne for me. So I don't want to marry him. I only say I am jealous; that is why I am going to Rome. If I stayed in Nice I could not work; I should only torment myself. Since knowing him, since he has paid me attention, my studies have suffered greatly, especially since it has seemed to me, and I am almost sure of it, that he is not madly in love with me, I have not been able to read a book or practise an hour on the piano.

Paris, November 18th, 1875.

Tired enough, finery will use me up, me and my money. But that is why I came to Paris, and we must do things conscientiously. I need not say that I am not having anything made in colours, everything is white.

I feel sad, unnerved, I should like to smile and to weep. No, really, love is full of interest.

I was in good spirits this evening, I talked with my aunt, and complained of M — — A — —. She answered that M — —A — — was a girl of the street, a worthless creature. I declared that she deserved every punishment for having, without knowing me, from mere gossip, formed a bad opinion of me and basely slandered me. Seizing a sheet of paper, I wrote:

"Contemptible old creature, your daughter no longer loves G — —, she loves a door-keeper in the Théâtre Italien, who is a very handsome fellow."

I sent this to D — —, who is going to mail it as if it came from Nice.

I wanted to howl this morning, but it would be too much like the dogs — I sigh and I laugh, which is amusing.

"Good Heavens," I said to my aunt yesterday, "do you suppose I could be in love? What I want is wealth. If my heart beats, it is when I see superb carriages, magnificent horses; if I am agitated, it is with the longing to have all these things.

"No, Madame, even if I loved any one, the luxury here would cure me very quickly. You don't know me, or you pretend not to know me."

I never spoke more truthfully; my aunt believed me, and began to comfort me; to calculate, to try to have money enough to satisfy my wants.

I worship people when they show good will. But the line of railroad that leads me to the Duc de H — — has made a tremendous curve! Yesterday he suddenly presented himself to my mind, so handsome that I am again completely captivated.

November 19th, 1875.

I have spent a day between L — — and W — —. It is full of interest, for dress forms an art, a talent, a science! Finery to this degree of perfection is a treat.

Oh, dear, how tiresome life is when one hasn't an income of at least 300,000 francs!

I have a dozen gowns made, a few hats, and stop there! It's absurd; one ought not to be embarrassed by such things. Oh, money, money! I must have it; I'll take any husband, if he will give it to me.

"And she has such ideas at fifteen," said my aunt.

"Yes, Aunt; not at fifteen; since I was thirteen-always."

"You are crazy," replied my aunt.

"I think so, too, but what is to be done?"

"If you don't sleep for ten nights wealth will not arrive any the more; come, go to bed; it's heartrending, heartrending."

"Madame, I must be married!"

"To E — —? No, indeed, he doesn't suit me."

I have written a lot of nonsense this evening; my ideas are very much confused, and the novel especially. And every time I talked seriously, my aunt was alarmed. Whenever I laughed, she laughed too.

Saturday, November 20th, 1875.

For three hours everything in the house has been in a state of revolution, but all the flames were extinguished in a business interview with D — —. With pride and confidence I assure myself that I am the wise head of the household. I believe that this time all the difficulties are smoothed, unless the matter is upset when I am no longer here.

Sunday, November 21st, 1875.

I want to return to Nice, the longer I stay here, the longer my departure for Rome is delayed. I spend my time in complaining; my aunt says I am crazy. I laugh, and so does she. Life is full of interest.

We went to my beautifiers, and also to B — —'s. To-morrow we shall decide upon the carriages. Then I went to see B — —, with whom I always keep up a correspondence. I spent an hour with her; we are not intimate friends, like young girls, we are mere acquaintances.

We received a letter from Mamma, with a clipping from a newspaper in which the opening of the opera at Nice was described, and a number of complimentary things said about us. So people are interested in me, but let us pass on. Mamma has been to the opera again, there was some mistake about the box, and old A — — came to give her a box by the side of his. Everybody came to see her-he was with Dina and O — —. Everybody enquired for us except G — —.

While reading this letter I committed a thousand extravagances, to the amazement of my aunt. Instantly taking a sheet of paper I wrote, disguising my hand, a letter to A — — D — —.

"Sir, here is a recent and true story from which your wonderful talent will be able to make a drama or a striking romance.

"A rich man, forty-five years old, married in Spain a young girl of sixteen and took her to his château in France. He was a widower, and had a son eight years old. This child, at the end of fifteen years, became a young man of three and twenty. He is handsome, impetuous, spoiled, but good and loyal. His stepmother is scarcely thirty-one, and beautiful. They love each other.

"Pursued by remorse, she could no longer endure the presence of her husband, who knew nothing. She planned that he should surprise her with some one else. The husband fired at her, but missed his aim.

"She fled to a convent where the husband is going to pursue her, wants to bring a lawsuit, take away her children-the oldest a girl of fifteen. The story could be turned to excellent account.

"There was also an interview between the young man and the woman, in which he sought to lead her into a reconciliation, showed her the scandal which this rupture would bring upon her daughters. It ended by a total separation, but if you wish you can kill off whichever you like, except the son, who is very well.

"Answer me through the correspondence of the Figaro, if you think there is anything in it, addressing the initials C.P.L."

"That is wicked and absurd," said my aunt.

"It is worse than wicked, worse than absurd, it is cowardly, but what do you expect, doesn't everybody know the story?"

"Yes, but people don't talk about it, not on account of the old man, who is a fool, whom everybody recognises as such, but for the sake of the young one, who is beloved. It is only since the son's appearance in society that his father has been let alone."

"Why does he look so fierce?" C — —asked B — — one day.

"Because so many stones have been thrown at him."

Wednesday, November 24th, 1875.

I slept for twelve hours and, while trying on at L——'s I felt ill. True, they kept me two hours with those wretched gowns.

We ordered from B—— a landau with eight springs, dark-blue, five seats, everything the very best, at the price of 6,000 francs; also a park phaeton of the same colour, the phaeton is for me. I already see myself in that little carriage, driving and saying: "Knowst thou the land —"

November 28th, 1875.

I am in Nice. From Paris to Lyon, we were in the midst of snow, but it is strange that I am not so delighted as I was before on reaching my villa.

At Toulon we met C — — and took her with us. Mamma and the S — —'s were waiting for us at the station. The grown-ups took a cab, and we entered our carriage.

We went to the opera. I wore a white barège costume made a little like a night-gown —open in front, as if by chance, and confined at the waist by a wide sash like a child's. We laughed heartily in spite of the general dulness.

I returned stupid, indifferent. It is the most detestable condition. I would rather weep. I don't love him. I hate him with all the strength with which I might have loved him. Nothing in the world effaces the resentment I have once felt.

Do you remember all that is wounding and terrible expressed in the one word "scorn"?

I understand, I who remember the slap my brother gave me more than twelve years ago, at whose recollection I am still as furious as if I had received it now; I who have kept a sort of hatred of my, brother on account of that childish affront. It was my only blow, but to make up for it, I have given a goodly number and to everybody. There was so much wickedness in my eyes that, when I looked in the glass, I was frightened by it. Everything can be pardoned except scorn. I would forgive a cruelty, a fit of passion, insults uttered in a moment of anger, even an infidelity, when people return and still love, but scorn —!

Monday, November 29th, 1875.

We went out at three o'clock. I who came to Nice in search of fine weather encountered Parisian cold. I wore an otter skin hat, made in the style of a baby hood, and my big sable pelisse covered with white cloth. The costume created a sensation, and my face did not look ugly, in spite of my fatigue.

I am so happy to be at home in my own house. I am sleeping in my big dressing room. My chamber will be ready in a month; I shall find it finished on my return from Rome. I am thinking only of that, of having my carriage, of spending a month in Nice, of continuing the studies I shall have begun in Rome, of following my professor's directions, and then of going to Russia. So many things have suffered, so much money has been lost because we failed to take our journey. There was a crowd to hear the band play. General B —— and V —— were near us. A —— was near the carriage.

"Are you going to stay long in Nice?"

"A week."

"Are you going away again?"

"Why, yes," replied my aunt.

"And where?"

"To Rome."

"Yes, to Rome," I added.

"But you do nothing but travel. Mademoiselle, you are a regular whirler."

"What a ridiculous man!"

We were walking, I, my aunt, and the General, who made me laugh by calling my attention to the different ways in which people looked at me, the men at my face, the women at my gown.

From this time I will no longer trouble myself about any one. I will become Galatea, let people love me, if they like!

I wonder why I am unhappy. No! I have no brains. Do people ask such things when they have? We are happy or we are unhappy, nothing does any good; neither prayer, nor tears, nor faith. I am a living proof, I lack everything.

When shall I go to Rome? I want to study, I am losing my time for nothing. If one does nothing, one ought to go into society; I am losing my time and I am bored.

O, misery of miseries! I will go all the same to pray to God, who knows?

While there is life, there is hope.

Saturday, December 4th, 1875.

I have told Mamma that I was going to study singing, and I shall do it, if it is God's pleasure to preserve my voice; it is the only way of gaining the fame for which I thirst, for which I would give ten years of my life without hesitation. I need renown, glory, and I will have them. *Deo juvante.* It has never happened that people wanted it, and did not have it! I have the most comprehensive ideas in the world. A fig for all that! Do I want it? A hundred times, no, a thousand times no! I was born to be a remarkable woman, it matters little in what way or how. All my tendencies are toward the great things of this world. I shall be famous, I shall be great, or I shall die!

It is impossible that God should have given me this *gloria cupiditis*, like S — —, for nothing, without an object; my time will come. I am happy when I think as I do to-day. Oh, my voice!

We went to the opera house to get a box for this evening. They gave the "Barber," my favourite little opera. I aspire to something unheard of, fabulous; I want to be famous, I will sing. It is queer, the whole Italian company saluted me. We were in No. 2. I wore my Empire gown, in which I like myself best. Hair dressed like an Olympian goddess, falling lower than the belt, and curled naturally at the ends. The General, always charming, was with us.

"Come," I said, "do you know what I am going to do?"

"What are you going to do, Mademoiselle?"

"I am going to make a mirror."

"How?"

"Look."

I took the attitude of old A — —, who sat opposite. He put his hand on the balustrade; I did the same. He leaned on his hand; I leaned on mine. He played with his chain; I played with my ribbon. He pulled his ear; I pulled mine.

The General laughed, Dina laughed, everybody laughed.

Every time he changed his position I imitated him like the most faithful mirror.

It was the last act, the house was half empty, and I continued my game in freedom till the last moment. I went out fairly jumping for joy and returned home gay and talkative.

To-night "Mignon" was given at the theatre.

I listened with pleasure and emotion. I forgot everything, toilette and audience, and, with my head resting against the pillar, I devoured the charming melodies. If I had "Mignon" given in my room I should enjoy it just as much, even more. With an interesting audience one hears nothing. I have seen this opera so many times! And I am always moved.

One could not imagine my impatience to go to Rome and resume my work. To study, to study, that is my desire! I grow joyous at the sight of my dear books, my adored classics, my beloved Plutarch.

I shall carry with me a few volumes to read, for I suppose we shall not see many people; we know no one there.

Saturday, December 11th, 1875.

The weather is magnificent. A tremendous crowd when we go out. We move at a walk, between hedges formed of the young men of Nice. They all take off their hats, and it seems as if I were the daughter of a queen whom they salute as she passes.

We met the Marvel, who alighted from his carriage and raised his hat to us twice. I was amused, I laughed, I went with O — —. Why did we laugh so much? I shall remember later.

Sunday, December 19th, 1875.

To-morrow there is to be a concert at the *Cercle de la Méditerranée* for the benefit of the free *École des beaux-arts*. I went to the club to get tickets. Entering through the big door I was ushered through well-heated, well-lighted corridors to the room of the secretary, who gave me the little book containing the by-laws and the names of the members. Men are lucky!

The club made a charming impression upon me. There is a fraternity of spirit a homelike air, which reminds one of the convent. I am no longer surprised that these men avoid their badly lighted, poorly heated homes, with household cares neglected, ill-disciplined servants, a wife in a wrapper and a bad humour, to go to a place where everything is nice, comfortable, elegant (in a land where the orange tree blossoms, where the breeze is softer and the bird swifter of wing).

O women, don't pity yourselves, but attend to your homes.

Long instructions might be given. I am content to say: "Make your house resemble a club as much as possible and treat your husbands as these ladies, L — —and C — —, treat them, and you will be happy and your husbands too."

Now I am calm and I think. O misery of miseries! O despair! What I have written expresses the best portion of what I feel. O God, have pity on me. Good people, do not jeer at me. Perhaps I give cause for amusement, but I am to be pitied. With my temperament, my ideas, I shall never explain what I feel. I shall never give an idea of my unhappiness, it is because while dying of shame, of scorn, of rage, I have the courage to jest. I really do have good health and a good disposition. Provided that what I have just said doesn't bring me misfortune!

I have a great many other things to say, but I am tired. I am going to write in big letters, "I am unhappy," and in letters still larger, "O God, aid me, have pity on me!"

These big letters represent an hour and a half of rage, tears, irritated self love, and two hours of prayer!

I have exhausted all words, I have exhausted my energy, I no longer have patience or strength, yet I still have one resource.

My voice. To preserve it I must take care of my health. Another week like this one, and good-bye to singing!

No, I will be sensible, I will pray to God. I will go to Rome. I am desperate, I will implore the Pope to pray for me. In my madness, I hope for that.

To-morrow I will talk with Mamma about my idea; aid me, my God.

Thursday, December 23d, 1875.

I am sorrowful and discouraged. My departure is an exile to me. I want to stay in Nice, and it is impossible. We always insist upon the impossible. The simplest thing, by resisting, gains in value.

Friday, December 24th, 1875.

B — — has been to our house. By a few words in the conversation he awoke in me so much love for Nice, so much regret at leaving, that I became unhappy and went to my room to sing-with such earnestness, such warmth, that I am still weeping from it-that eternal air, and these delightful words:

> "Alas! Would it were possible I might return,
> Unto that vanished land whence I was torn,
> There, there alone to live my heart doth yearn,
> To live, to love, to die."

How I pity those who are not like me! They do not understand how much truth there is in this familiar fragment that is sung in every drawing-room. Yes, *there alone to live my heart doth yearn.* Yes, at Nice, in my beloved villa. People may go through the world. They will find sublime landscapes, impressive mountains, frightful gulfs, wild beauties of nature, picturesque towns, great cities; but, on returning to Nice one would say that elsewhere it was beautiful, magnificent! but here it is pleasant, attractive, congenial; here one wants to stay; here one is alone and surrounded, hidden and in sight, as one desires. Nowhere else does one breathe as freely, as joyously. Nowhere else is there this extraordinary blending of the real and the artificial, the simple and the exquisite! Finally, what shall I say? Nice is my city. I am going, but I shall return.

> Go, but still regret it,
> Regret has its charms,

as one of the pleasant simpletons called poets has said.

To-morrow will be Christmas, and I am planning a joke with C — —. We are going to buy a pair of huge slippers, a jockey, reins for driving (suitable for a child), and two little sheep. We will put these things into the slippers, make a package, and under the cord slip a letter written in this form:

"Santa Claus has found little E — —very good, and hopes he will continue to be. The toys are for little E — —, the slippers for little 'papa.'" And on the envelope one may guess what. But we shall not send it, Dina is going to disguise herself as a boy, and, with her blue spectacles and pale complexion, she appears like a professor of mathematics. C — — and I will also make ourselves unrecognisable and, at eight o'clock, go to the club, and tell the coachman to give the package to the janitor from M. E — —. We laughed as we used to do. What amuses me is to see a serious woman play pranks with me.

This morning we had a call from a Sister T — —. She left two visiting cards. *The Sisters of the Good Shepherd.* I took one, added P.P.C. and, with an address written on it, sent it to Tour.

Saturday, December 25th, 1875.

Ah! son felica! Ah! son rapita!

Find me a language which expresses thought with so much enthusiasm. So I use it to define my condition. It is heavenly weather, everybody is out of doors, in spite of my vigil yesterday, I look pretty.

I go to walk enchanted, happy, I sing "Mignon" softly and everything seems beautiful to me. Everybody looks at me so pleasantly, those whom I know salute me. I should like to hug them all. Oh, how comfortable we are in Nice, I should not want to go away.

I have a longing for amusement, I should like to invite everybody to the house, to give a dinner, a ball, a supper, a reception, to have some sort of diabolical carnival —I should like to have everybody, everybody. I am not ill-natured at heart, I am only a little crazy.

Ah! son felica! Ah! son rapita
Dio Virgina Sanctissima.

We went to the opera, Mamma and I in the 3d box in the first row, my aunt and Dina in the 2nd next to the Marvel. T — — came in, General B — — was with us. The door opened and the Marvel appeared.

"Well," said I, "you celebrated Christmas."

"Ah! yes, just think, I received a pair of slippers."

"Slippers!"

"Yes, and mine were so worn out that they came very opportunely, and an anonymous letter which was not signed-that is very natural, anonymous letters are never signed. And the same day I received a letter, a visiting card: *The Sisters of the Good Shepherd.*"

Everybody laughed.

"What does P.P.C. mean?" I asked.

"Pays Parting Calls."

"Oh, yes, that's true."

"But for some time I have received a great many things, the other day a bit of broken rock, pierced by an arrow. All the people in the box shouted with laughter, and so did I. But I saw plainly that he was furiously angry and suspected everything. It is terrible that only the most foolish little pranks should be remembered."

"You are very fortunate, I received nothing at all."

"Ah! If you wish, I'll send you some slippers."

"But if they are so big, what should I do with them?"

"Never mind, I'll send you all the things."

"That is kind, I am quite overpowered."

BOOK LI

From Sunday, December 26th, to Sunday, January 9th, 1876; Nice, Promenade des Anglais, 55 bis, in my villa. —From Monday, January 3d, in Rome, Hôtel de Londres, Piazza di Spagna.

Sunday, December 26th, 1875.

We went to hear the band. G. M — — came to talk to us and, among other compliments, said to me: "M — —, I would like to give you some of my experience, I love you so much! No, really, Madame," —addressing my mother —"she has such an extraordinary mind, so developed, so broadened. But it lacks experience. M — —, my child, I will give you some advice."

"Give it, Monsieur, give it."

"Well, never love seriously, for there not in me whole world a man worthy your love."

"Yes, I know that. I know that men are not equal to women. You are not equal to your wife, I can tell you."

"You are right, M — —."

He is right. I shall never love wholly. I shall worship, I shall rave, I shall commit follies and even, if opportunity offers, have a romance. But I shall not love, for candidly in my inmost heart, I am convinced of the villainy of men. Not only that, I do not find any one worthy of my love, either morally or physically. It is useless to say and think all I want. A — — will never be anything but a good-looking member of the fashionable society of Nice —a gay liver, almost a fop. Oh, no; every man has some defect that prevents loving him entirely. One is stupid, another awkward, another ugly, another-in short, I seek physical and moral perfection.

Now that it is two o'clock in the morning, that I am shut up in my room, wrapped in my long white dressing-gown, my feet bare and my hair down, like a virgin martyr, I can give myself up to a throng of bitter reflections. I shall go, carrying in my heart all the sorrowful and wicked things that can be contained there.

December 28th, 1875.

I don't want public pity, but I should like to have one creature to understand me, compassionate me, weep with me sincerely, knowing why she was weeping, seeing with me into the farthest corner of my heart. What is there more dastardly, more ugly, viler than mankind?

Wednesday, December 29th, 1875.

We went to see Mme. du M — —. She gave me seven letters of introduction for Rome. May God grant that they will be of the service this excellent woman desires, she loves me so much! No doubt everybody has trouble. One is ill, another is in love, another wants money, another is bored. You will say, perhaps, "Poor little idler, she thinks she is the only person who is unhappy, while she is happier than most people." But my sorrow is the most hateful of all.

We lose a beloved one. We mourn for a year, two years, and remain sorrowful all our lives. The greatest grief loses its force with time, but an incessant, eternal torment!...

I have just read Mme. du M — —'s letters. No one could be kinder, no one could be more charming. And, just think, the greater part of the time those who would like to do things cannot. It is six years since she left Rome and I doubt whether her acquaintances remember her; and then, her influence was never great.

> "Have you suffered, wept, and languished,
> Thinking hope was all in vain,
> Soul in mourning, torn heart anguished?
> Then you understand my pain."

Sappho was given to-night. I wore a sort of Neapolitan shirt of blue crêpe de Chine and old lace, with a white front. It can't be described-it was as original and charming as possible, with a white skirt and an alms-bag of white satin. We arrived at the end of the first act, and were near P — — and R — —, and I heard the voice of the Marvel. Nothing can be said against her face, it is blooming; whether real or artificial is of little consequence. She has hair-oh, I don't know. At Spa, she was fairer than I; here, she is darker

> *"d'un serpent, jaune et sifflant."*

Now the American has gone home, and is doubtless in a sleep which will preserve her twenty-seven-year-old complexion, while I am awake. Just now I fell on my knees sobbing, beseeching God, with my arms outstretched, my eyes fixed on space before me, exactly as if God was there in my room. I believe I am uttering insolent things to God.

The S — —'s came, and after dinner we began to tell fortunes and laughed almost as much as we did before, that is, the others did, but I could not. Then we poured melted wax into cold water (it is the shadow that is looked at). I had in succession a lion couchant with one of his front paws extended, holding a rose; isn't it odd? Then a great heap of something surmounted by a garland held by Cupids.

As for M — —, her wax figure cast a horrible shadow. A woman lying as if dead with her hands crossed on her breast. O — — and Dina had insignificant shadows. And, at fifteen minutes before midnight, four mirrors were brought, two for Dina and two for me, and we took up the great fortune telling.

I looked with all my eyes, without stirring, almost without breathing. In the proper costume of night-gown and unbound hair. But everything was very vague; it quivered, danced, formed, and reformed every instant.

Saturday, January 1st, 1876.

Here is the new year. Greeting and mercy. Well, the first day of 1876 was not so bad as I expected. They say the whole year is spent very much like the first day, and it is true. I spent the first of last January in the cars, and I have really travelled a great deal.

To-morrow, yes, to-morrow I shall be glad to go. I am perfectly happy, for I have made a plan—a plan that will fail like the others, but which amuses me in the meanwhile. If it were not two o'clock in the morning, I would write a whole story of the sale of a soul. The brutes—I have not wept, I have not felt sad once. A very pleasant day to commence the year. I shall go and think only of returning. No doubt I shall change my mind in Rome. All the same, this is where I should like to live.

I had already closed my book, but I and a lot of things to say. I have looked at the great caricature, there are five of us. I have thought of everything; of Mme. B — —, of the English, of the people of Nice, of S — —, of "Mignon." In a word, a quantity of things. I had a great deal to say, and lo! I stop.

It is tiresome to go, but it is horrible to stay. P — — has dramatic emotions so genuine that she delights and thrills me. Come, what was I going to write? That I am calm and agitated, sorrowful and joyous, jealous and indifferent. It seems to me that fastidious society is possible to have and, at the same time, it is impossible.

> "I wish to stay and I wish to go,
> How it will end I do not know."

I cannot lie down. I am sorrowful, excited.

Oh, calm yourself, for Heaven's sake. It hasn't anything to do with M. A — —, but simply that I am going. The uncertainty, the vagueness, leaving the known for the unknown.

Sunday, January 2nd, 1876.

"I shall go Sunday at three o'clock," I said or rather shrieked, and Sunday at one o'clock everything was topsy-turvy. The trunks were still empty, and the floor was covered with gowns and finery. For my part, I put on a grey dress and waited quietly. C — — and Dina worked, and so well that everything was ready for the hour of departure.

At half past two, C — — and I got into a little cab and went to hear the band, and I listened once more to the municipal music of Nice. "Come," I said to Collignon, "if this piece is gay, our journey will be, too. I am superstitious." And the piece was very lively. So much the better!

I saw G — —, who bid me good-bye once more. I haven't seen the Marvel, but that doesn't matter.

We got into the landau again, and went to the station. Our friends came there, one after another. I skipped about, I laughed, I chattered like a bird. How kind they are, and how hard it is to leave them.

"You feign this gaiety," said B — —to me, "but in your heart you are weeping, I am sure of it." "Ah! you think so? No!

"When to Nice you bid good-bye,
Unfeigned joy is in your eye.
Easy 'tis from Nice to part,
For she never wins your heart."

"Bravo! Bravo!"

The quatrain was made one evening when we were capping verses with G — —.

"Give me some cigarettes," I said softly to my aunt.

"Very well, later."

I thought she had forgotten, but at Monaco she wrapped a number in paper and gave them to me. She, who cries out when I ask her for them at home. At Monaco we parted, and those horrid cigarettes made me cry. I was sorry for the poor old grandfather, my aunt, everybody. I am vexed to have to go with Mamma. I was with her at Spa and, besides, I am used to my aunt.

Oh! torture! Imagine the tediousness of a journey in Italy. Mamma and Dina do not know Italian. I refused to use my tongue; I can scarcely use my limbs. By dint of complaining because I was not with my aunt, and saying: "Who asked you to come with us? I ought to go with my aunt. Why do you come with me?" I obtained a passive obedience and an alacrity impossible to imagine.

Night found us in a car. I complained, wept softly, and said the most provoking things to my mother, like the brute I am.

At last, toward three o'clock, Monday, January 3d, ruins, columns, aqueducts began to appear on the dreary plain called the Roman Campagna, and we entered the station of Rome. I saw nothing, I heard nothing. I was utterly limp after these twenty-four hours without sleep.

We were taken to the Hôtel de Londres, Piazza di Spagna, and we occupied an apartment on the ground floor, with a yellow drawing-room that was very fresh and neat, I was tired and depressed, in the condition in which I needed some one to sustain me. And Mamma was crying. Oh, dear!

We must set to work very, very quickly to look about us. There is nothing I hate like changing.

New streets, strange faces, and no Mediterranean. Only the miserable Tiber. I am utterly wretched when I am in a new city. I shut myself up in my room to collect my scattered wits a little.

Tuesday, January 4th, 1876.

Yesterday Mamma wrote to B — —, the brother of the empress's physician, and to-day he came to our house. He devotes himself to painting. After this visit, we went out. Oh! the ugly city, the impure air! What a deplorable mixture of ancient magnificence and modern filth!

We went through the Corso, the Via Gregoriana, the Forum of Hadrian, the Forum of Rome, we saw the gates of Septimus Severus, and Constantine, the Via Pia, the Coliseum, but everything is still vague, I don't recognise myself. The drive on the Pincio is charming, the band was playing, but there were not many people when we were there. Statues, statues everywhere. What would Rome be without statues? From the summit of the Pincio we looked at the dome of St. Peter and also the whole city. I am glad to find it is not over large, it will be easier to know.

On the drive we were amused to meet the S — —'s, A — —, and P — — of Rome. The sun did not appear, and the weather was dull and dreary.

On arriving in Rome, I had no artistic feeling. It is Rome that opened my mind, so I have worshipped her since. I don't want to visit anything before we are settled. The evening was spent in consulting the cards and in writing letters.

This stay in Rome seems an exile and it is with unequalled joy that I think of returning to Nice. The cards predict much good, but can the cards be believed?

Ah! if I could marry some prince! Then I would return to Nice and make a triumphal entry. But no, it is indicated that nothing will succeed for me; so I shall make no more plans or, if I do, it will be with the sorrowful conviction of their uselessness. Each time I have been disappointed.

Wednesday, January 5th, 1876.

This is what I wrote to the General:

"I am in Rome, and it is very wonderful (ah! it is very wonderful, very marvellous). It is cold as Russia, the water freezes in the fountains, but the cold would be nothing if it was *only* the cold. Since morning we have been in search of an apartment, and we have seen only one. I did not have courage to go up when they pointed out a black, yawning hole, dirty and frightful. I have looked in vain for a house with any resemblance to the French houses. I find only ruins or cracked columns. No doubt it is very beautiful, but agree with me that a good, comfortable apartment is infinitely more pleasant, though less artistic.

"I believe we shall end by lodging in the baths of Caracalla or in the Coliseum. The foreigners will take me for the ghost of a Christian martyr, devoured by some fierce tiger in the presence of some carnivorous emperor. As to the furniture, we will be content with fragments of statues or a few bones, the sublime remains of a henceforth impossible past. After my installation in the Coliseum, or in the Forum, I will give you the most minute details concerning the Eternal City. Meanwhile, I shall expect a letter from you, my dear General, which will be, I know, kind and charming. Now good-bye until we meet again.

MARIE BASHKIRTSEFF."

It is the truth, there is not a habitable apartment; where are we? Can this horrible city be called a capital? We are not in Europe! Not a house fit to rent. I am discouraged, tired, but I will not stir before May.

O Rome! I think that we shall take a larger apartment in the hotel, and stay there. One can breathe only in the Piazza di Spagna. It is impossible that this is Rome! What a mixture of beautiful antiquities and modern trash!

Thursday, January 6th, 1876.

B — — has been here again and brought the addresses of some professors. Then we took a carriage, and Mamma went to the Russian priest's, the archimandrite Alexander. Being an archimandrite, he is married, for in our country priests and deacons can be married once. Mamma says that he is charming. Our embassy makes no show, and has not even any regular reception day.

This society makes me love Rome. I scarcely regret Nice, the ungrateful, wicked city.

Sad and irresolute yesterday, I am gay and confident to-day. I have written to my aunt to send me F — —, the ugly little negro will be very nice to have here.

I have had a good dinner, and spent the evening in reading the history of Charles the Bold.

I thought, "in my ingenuous candour," that there was no society except in Nice, but there is a great deal, and even very excellent.

After the drive we went down the Corso, thronged with carriages, between rows of pedestrians of all classes. D — —was among them. Now that my eyes are opened to see the beauties and antiquities of Rome, I am growing curious, eager to visit everything. I am no longer drowsy. I am in a hurry to be everywhere. I want to live at full speed again. Ah! if only I could!... Again a longing for Nice. The poorest thing, by resisting, gains worth. Be thoroughly convinced of this genuine truth. Do not believe that I am stupefied to the point of not seeing beyond the city of S — —; on the contrary, I am more ambitious than ever. But meanwhile, to spit upon some one who has spit on us, to give the person a kick, is a pleasure which every well-born soul can permit itself.

Friday, January 7th, 1876.

Goodness! What prices people ask in Rome! For 1,800 francs one has only the barest necessaries! At the Hôtel de Rome I saw an apartment so large and so fine that it made my head ache. In France we have no idea of this grandeur, this ancient majesty. After much searching we have taken an apartment in the second story of the Hôtel de Londres, with a balcony looking out upon the Piazza di Spagna, a handsome drawing-room, several bedrooms, and a study. We went to B——'s studio. He has very fair talent.

Tuesday, January 11th, 1876.

We did not go out, but the artist Kalorbinski came, and to-morrow the lessons will begin. Monseigneur de Faloux, being unable to go out himself, sent the Chevalier Rossy to bring us a number of pleasant messages. I received him. I have learned a great deal about affairs in the city.

I am very proud of receiving some one myself. It seems like a sovereign's first decree. The Russian priest has come to call on us too. I like the cowled monks in Rome. They are new to me, and that pleases me.

At last I have a teacher of painting; that is something. This evening I see everything in rose-colour, and I am already thinking of a letter in which it will be said of A — —: *Et eum dicat super malitiosum, improbum, inhonestum, cupidum, luxuriosum, ebriosum!* Exactly what Septimus Severus said of Albinus.

If only the winter would pass more quickly. With all my misfortunes, I feel better in Nice, I can give myself up to despair as much as I please. Only last Spring, there was nobody there. The best people gathered around us. P — — was deserted, so were the others. While this Spring there will again be nobody, but P — — will have Miss R — —. These ladies, under the leadership of T — —, will form a sort of court, like that of the young Princess G — — and Mme. T — — three months since. Both died three months ago.

We shall see. Meanwhile let us study, and try to go into society. Let us pray to God, and amuse ourselves by writing letters.

Wednesday, January 12th, 1876.

B — — and his cousin have called to see us. When these Russians go, I put on my dressing gown again, and say a lot of things, and rank myself among the goddesses, then descend to calling myself a little bundle of dirty linen.

I like to indulge in extravagant speeches, and make Mamma laugh. I received a letter from B — —, this charming friend gives me the news of Nice. P — —has had a reception, and everybody went. It seems that we were mentioned in the presence of quite a large number of persons in the consul's house, and the consul and his wife said nothing but good about us.

"I was glad," B — — wrote, "to see that they were your friends, too, though you no longer went there so often."

After all, I am very happy, very calm, and I am going to bed.

Thursday, January 13th, 1876.

Mamma and Dina are at church. It is our New Year's Day, and I have stayed at home to sew. That is my whim at present, and I must do what I wish. B — — called to offer his good wishes.

Not until four o'clock did they succeed in dragging me out of the house and, at five o'clock. Mamma is going to the embassy. That is the hour Baronne D — —receives.

We had a telegram from Barnola. He congratulates us, and reminded me of the promise I made to drink a glass of water at the Fountain of Trevi at two o'clock on the Russian New Year's Day. He vowed friendship, I did the same.

I received a letter from my aunt, in which she told me that A — — was paying attention to an English girl whom she has nicknamed Olive. My aunt has so lively an imagination. At the end of three days of our acquaintance with the Marvel, she told me that the poor fool was in love with me. And she pitied him with eager kindness while predicting for him the fate of the Polish count. Now she has seen him at Monaco with the girl, and she is already marrying them. Oh! it is really atrocious-always conjectures! Ah! if I could know the truth. Have patience, that is easy to write. But to show it! Patience is the virtue of sluggish-but gentle, foolish souls.

I don't think I love the Marvel, I don't find him in my heart; but at any rate, the surface is very much occupied with him. If he loved me, I shouldn't care very much, that is the truth.

Friday, January 14th, 1876.

We met on the Pincio Count B — —, who started at seeing me, then bowed to my mother.

At five o'clock we went to see Monseigneur F — —, a thin, black, agile old priest in a wig, a Jesuit, a hypocrite. He received us very courteously in his remarkable drawing-rooms, filled with things in the best taste. Gobelins, pictures, and all this in the dwelling of a detestable Jesuit. Well, well!

We all went to walk in the Villa Borghese, which is more beautiful than the Doria. There was a crowd of people, and the pretty Princess M — — was walking like any ordinary mortal, followed by her carriage, with the coachman and two footmen in red livery. This quantity of carriages with coats of arms saddened me. We know nobody, God help me! Perhaps I am ridiculous with my complaints, and my eternal prayers! I am so miserable! This evening Mamma asked the date of last year's carnival; I took out my journal and, without noticing it, spent two hours turning over the leaves.

I said to myself: I am living to be happy! Everything must bow before me! And see how it is-the idea that I could fail in anything never occurred to me.

A delay, yes, but a complete failure, nonsense! —And I see with terror and humiliation that I was deceived, that nothing happens as I wish. It is not because I love some one; I do not love anybody seriously; I love a coronet and money. It is terrible to think that everything is escaping. Each instant I long to pray to God, and each instant I stop myself. I shall pray again, let what will happen!

My God, Holy Virgin, do not scorn me, take me under your protection.

Sunday, January 16th, 1876.

I feel that I shall write badly, for I have just been reading my old journal. Mamma begged me to read the period of G——. I read it, passing over a number of things. What is perfectly simple when written is no longer so when read aloud. My face burned, my fingers grew cold, and I ended by saying that I could not go on.

"She will read it to us in two years," said Mamma.

After St. Peter's, Mamma went to Baron d'I——'s, the ambassador's cousin. She made his acquaintance at the ambassadress's. These people are very simple and agreeable. I liked the baron especially.

There was a crowd on the Pincio, the Corso and the Piazza Colonna were thronged with carriages and people returning from the Pincio.

We dined at the table d'hôte because the son of the Grand Duke of Baden was to dine there. A number of society people were present, and the Grand Duke is a pleasant fellow enough-for a Grand Duke.

Wednesday, January 19th, 1876.

We went to the Pincio, there were a great many people. The Duc de L — —, son of the Grand Duchess M — —, the emperor's sister, was there with Mme. A — —, the wife of a Russian prefect. The Duc de L — — saw her and was captivated. Since then she is always with him. It is said that they are secretly married and live abroad. That is what people call having happiness. She had liveried servants and magnificent horses-suitable, I should think, for the niece of the Emperor of Russia.

January 19th, 1876.

At the church of St. John we met Baronne d'I — —, the ambassadress's cousin, who came up to Mamma and talked with her a long time, apologising for not having yet called, on account of her husband's illness. Mamma went to her house last Sunday, three days ago.

From there to the Pincio, then to the Corso, crowds everywhere, I like this animation.

My aunt wrote that the Marvel, but she doesn't call him that, everybody at Nice in our house calls him nothing but the "shaved magpie," so my aunt wrote that the "shaved magpie" was at the opera, and did nothing all the evening but weep, actually weep.

There is news from Russia, nothing good, I think of nothing but praying to God, and am in fear.

I pity myself *now*, what would it be if we should lose our fortune! Horrible!

I pray to God and tremble. God will not abandon me.

* * * * *

Rome bores me; Nice is my beloved country. I see Rome, Paris, London, kings, courts, but there is nothing so pretty as my dear villa. If ever I am rich, titled, and happy, I shall not forget it. I shall spend several months of the year there! no, several months —I could not do that, for everywhere, except in London, winter is the principal season.

We went to the photographer, S — —'s, to tell him that I would come to pose on Monday. I saw there a number of portraits of people I know. While looking at L — —, his wife, and L — — D — —, it seemed as if he were going to bow to me. Then a bewitching woman with big, deep eyes, and heavy eyebrows above a straight nose. She resembles R — —. Dina says it is she. But no, she has not that round chin with a dimple, and those magnificent eyes. No, it can't be, she is not so beautiful.

Then to the Pincio, then to a milliner to order a Marie Stuart cap, and a Marie Antoinette turban. The woman showed me a gown she was making for a ball at the Quirinal, day after to-morrow.

This plunges me into inconceivable torture. If you knew how I dread spending the Carnival without a single amusement! We found the ambassadress's card at our home, so she has returned the visit. It is rather late, all the same. Her cousin came at dinner time. The Grand Duke of L — — asked who we were (who is that pretty Russian?). B — — says Mamma ought to go to call on the Marquise de M — —. He says it is the custom here, especially from a foreigner to a Roman lady. Let Mamma go anywhere, provided that I can go where I like. My torture has no bounds, I am dying of it every instant. Do you want a proof of my despair? There are times when I hope to marry A — — and be something at Nice with P — —; that gives the measure of my discouragement, my desperation.

I have had this humiliating thought once or twice. I tell you to show you how low I descend, how vexed, how martyrised I am to live in this way. Who will restore my lost time, my best time? I have used every expression, and am dying because I cannot make myself understood.

I have written to C — — and to B — —. I was in a hurry to tell them the good news. I have the very weak middle notes which accompany the abnormal compass of my voice. I have found a method of singing that strengthens them wonderfully, so that they are almost as strong as the rest. This delights me, and I am eager to write about it to B — —, who is so much interested in my voice. But for that, it would have required two years study to render them satisfactory. I thank God, and will pray to Him for the other things.

Thursday, January 20th, 1876.

After three years study, if no accident happens, I shall have a voice such as is rarely heard, and I shall not yet be twenty.

F —— is severe and just.

I am afraid to say all that I think of my voice; a strange modesty closes my lips. Yet I have always spoken of myself as if I were talking of some one else, which has perhaps made people think me blind and arrogant.

Friday, January 21st, 1876.

I want to have a gown like the one worn by Dante's Beatrice.

Saturday, January 22nd, 1876.

Still another proof of the falsity of the cards. Yesterday I had a sort of sorceress come and she pretended to give me good luck. She told me to call the person I wanted. I called A —— and that woman told me he could not live without me; that he was dying of grief and jealousy, and he was especially jealous because a wicked woman had told him that I loved another man.

May all the witches die! May all the cards burn! They are nothing but lies!

Sunday, January 23d, 1876.

I am making a large white garment for the house, for the spring, in Nice. Nice, miserable city, why cannot I live there as I like? In Nice I know everybody, but to live in Nice except as a queen isn't worth while.

I am sad, I am in a foreign country, I long to return home, just for a single day, for if I stayed longer, I should want to go back.

In the evening we went to the Apollo theatre, they gave the *Vestal* and a ballet. I wore white with a Greek coiffure. There were a great many people, and an especially large number of men. Not a single woman between our box and the stage.

From Monday, January 24th, to February 10th, 1876: Rome, Hôtel de Londres, Piazza di Spagna.

I swear that all these tragic and jealous remarks about A — — were written under the influence of romantic reading, and that I only half believed them while I was writing, exciting myself for the pleasure of it, and I greatly regret these exaggerations.

The archimandrite has been at our house. He is a charming man who, after having been a soldier, turned monk from despair at having lost his wife. He told us that there was a Madame S — — who greatly desired to make Mamma's acquaintance.

Returning from the photographer's, such dismal thoughts filled my brain that I did not dress and let Mamma and Dina go out without me. Being left alone, I am very sad, I am singing "Mignon."

Tuesday, January 25th, 1876.

I am homesick. I took a singing lesson, and then went out with Mamma. We went to M. de E——'s studio. He requested permission to present a very elegant and popular M. Benard, received everywhere in society. He told us a great many things about Rome.

From there we went to Monseigneur de F——'s, who yesterday asked if we had had our audience.

This priest is turning out better and better, he has even made scandals. He told us that I had been noticed at the opera, my white dress had attracted attention, and said that to go to court we need only write to the Minister or Ambassador.

"I should like," he added, "to be able to open to you the other door, as I have opened the Holy One."

"O Monseigneur," I replied, "the Holy Door is far preferable."

From there to the residence of Madame S —— (the archimandrite had told her, and she was expecting us), who is the most charming and the ugliest woman in the world. She received us in the most delightful way, and immediately spoke of the Quirinal.

Footnotes

1.   *La Légende d'une cosmopolite.*
2.   Marie Bashkirtseff's governess.

Made in the USA
Monee, IL
16 June 2026

54284203R00046